Devi

The Divine Goddess

James H. Bae

MANDALA
PUBLISHING
San Rafael

MANDALA
PUBLISHING

17 Paul Drive
San Rafael, CA 94903
Tel: 415.883.4055
Orders: 800.688.2218
Website: www.mandala.org
Email: info@mandala.org

ISBN: 978-1-60109-022-5

Designed & Printed by Palace Press International
Printed in China

Contents

Introduction

In Hindu Mythology, Devi is known as the Divine Goddess. She appears in many guises and is the Divine Mother and Creator from which all female deities are formed. Devi is worshiped by millions in all her many aspects. As the consort of Shiva, she appears as Sati and Parvati. She is love, spiritual fulfillment, beauty and the beloved of Krishna, Sri

Radha. Of abundance, fortune and virtue, she is Lakshmi, wife of Narayana. Devi is the dark and ferocious Kali, who slays the evils of ignorance in order to bring forth new insights. Devi has a special role in the Hindu pantheon as Creator, Preserver and Destroyer; she is magnificent in all her manifestations. ■

Devi as the Divine Feminine

Perhaps the most vital component of Indian metaphysics is the understanding that life is built on the principles of both masculine and feminine counterparts. This is embodied in the notions of shakitman and shakti. The term shaktiman refers to the masculine counterpart of divinity, the Godhead who is the personification of omnipotence.

Devi manifests as Shakti—the Divine Feminine, the Goddess from whom the power and abundance of the Divine Whole is displayed in the natural world. The divine feminine is the source of all potentiality; creativity and ability in life and all the spheres of existence derive their quality from her. She is the world, the self and the ability to perceive. ■

The Goddess
and Artistic Creation

One way we can visualize this is in the genesis of art, which itself can serve as a great model and expression of the universal dynamics of life. Inspiration and revelation are inherently dynamics of consciousness and they are also the fundamental source of the artist's creative acts. According to the metaphysical understanding of Shiva-Shakti, consciousness is to be considered a masculine principle. Shiva, the embodiment of nondual consciousness, reveals himself through his divine counterpart, Shakti. Thus, "cluing one into a more profound vision of life" by revelation in the heart and mind of the artists can only come about through the agency of the divine feminine. Therefore, knowledge and revelation are the work of the Goddess.

Beyond the creative intuition of the artists, there are the organic elements he or she employs in the making of art. The minerals used in making paints, the elements that make up the brush and canvas and prana, or fundamental life energy, which activates the functions of the mind and body to deliver that primary intuition, are all made possible by the energy of the divine feminine. The physical experience of art through the senses and intellect of the audience is also granted by the Goddess. Thus, consciousness plays an active and integral part in our waking experiences via Shakti. For all beings alike, not only the mystic and artist, she is the force that allows us to approach all of our life endeavors. ■

The Many Forms
of the Goddess

In India, the Goddess plays a most notable
role in the spiritual geography of the
land. There is multiplicity of female
deities worshipped, all of whom are
regarded as aspects of the one divine
mother.

Divya Dehejia writes:

She is encountered in manifold guises. In a simple wooden shrine in the town of Chatradi in the Himalayan foothills she stands as a glowing brass image, smooth and sensuous, adorned with jewels and silks. On a hilltop near Guwahati in north-eastern Assam, worshipers invoke her presence in the simple form of a cleft in a natural boulder filled with water from an underground spring. At the Kalighat shrine in Calcutta (from Kalikatta, literally, seat of Kali), priests drape her so as to reveal only a fierce face with three golden

eyes and a large protruding golden tongues above which are engraved her upper lip and set of teeth: four silver arms emerge from the drapery, two holding a sword and severed head, the others blessing the devotee. In Nepal, worshipers invoke her in a beautiful living child dressed in red (referring to an honored institution of worshiping Kumaris, virgins, in whom the goddess Durga resides for propitiation), with eyes dramatically outlines with collyrium, a third eye painted prominently on her forehead, and hair piled up in an elaborate topknot. She is a bizarre, fiendish figure riding a wild ass with a third

eye in its flank in Tibet; in southern
Madurai, she is a dark stone figure
concealed beneath crown jewels, silks,
and flowers. And in the numerous
villages of the Indian subcontinent,
she is little more than a vermilion-
smeared stone or mound of earth.
In all these guises, and many others,
devotees address her as Devi (Great
Goddess) and Ma (Mother).[1]

The Goddess in her archetype as the
Divine Mother embodies all that exists
in the manifest creation. Jung refers to
this archetype as "Intimately known
and yet strange like Nature, lovingly
tender and yet cruel like fate, joyous and

untiring giver or life—mater dolorosa, and mute implacable portal that closes upon the dead."[2] The mother is the very tree of life from which all life forms spring. And as life is diversified, the role of mother takes many forms. In

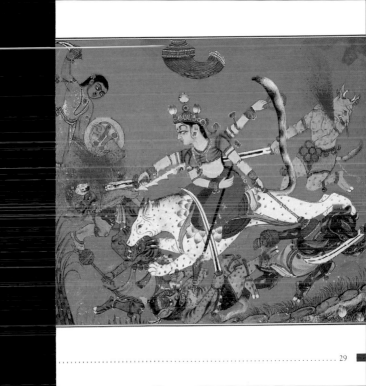

the horrific form of Kali, for example, she personifies the natural process of destruction. Toward evil, she slays the demons of ignorance. Her appearance may seem frightening to those unfamiliar with her image, but just as death is inevitable and destruction a certainty for anything which is created in the world, the Hindu perspective on this aspect of the divine is not an entirely fearful one. Kali is indeed one of Devi's more wrathful forms. Alain Danielou lists these twelve notable features of her image: The corpse, a fearful appearance, a haunting laugh, four arms, a sword, a severed head, the fear-removing hand, the giving hand, an infamous garland of

Of all her manifestations, Devi is best known in her role as the consort of Lord Shiva. Her benevolent nature is personified in Uma (light one), Sati (the chaste), Gauri (golden or brilliant) and Parvati (the goddess of the mountain). However, she is also Chandi (fierce), Kali (the dark one and the form of time), Bhairavi (consort of Bhairava or "the terrible"), Durga (the terrible) and Ambika (the divine mother).

One popular image of Durga is represented with the skulls of asuras garlanding her neck. In her left hand she holds the khadga, a weapon she uses to devour enemies. War is a manifestation of Durga's wrath, by

which she frees the world of negative influences. Durga also reveals a benign aspect to her devotees, as an affectionate mother who wisely rebukes and teaches them determination in spiritual life.

Goddess worship, more commonly known as Shaktism, was not a prominent tradition in the time of the early Vedic religion. In the epic period, Devi (the Goddess) figures more prominently in the life of Hindus and Shaktism becomes a principal component of the religious life of the Indian subcontinent. Between the fifth and sixth centuries, the Devi Mahatmya, part of the Markandeya Purana, emerges as a principal religious script, clearly presenting the preeminent position of the Goddess, not only in her role in creation, but also depicting her as the Supreme Being.

David Kinsley, in his work on the Goddess in Hindu mythology, discussed the theology of the Devi Mahatmya:

> The theology underlying Durga's [an epithet for the goddess meaning "the terrible"] cosmic interventions and the structure of the demon-

slaying myths conform to well-known Hindu ideas and forms. The idea of a deity's role to balance and uphold the cosmic order is a central Vaishnavite idea. Ever since the time of the Bhagavad Gita, the idea of Vishnu's descent in the world has been widely accepted in the Hindu tradition. Durga, the Devi Mahatmya, is heir to this avatara theology. In fact, in many ways Durga is a female version of Vishnu. She, like him, creates, maintains and destroys the world and intervenes on a cosmic scale whenever disorder, or the appearance of certain demons, threaten to disrupt the world. She is approached by the other gods as their savior in times of distress. This conformity to a well-known type of theology does not detract from Durga's appeal, power, or prestige. On the contrary, by creating her in this familiar role and by telling her myths according to a familiar structure, the author of the Devi Mahatmya underlines Durga's supremacy and might.[5]

The first cycle of this classic religious script narrates the story of Brahma, the creator god and how he is threatened by two demons, Madhu and Kaitabha. In numerous accounts, Brahma implores

Vishnu to descend to the world and to put an end to the suffering caused by such demons. Here Vishnu is described as reclining on his support, the serpent Shesa Naga and remaining in slumber. It is only through the power of Devi that he can be awakened and spurred into activity. The Brahma utters a hymn to the Goddess, for it is she who can release Vishnu from mahamaya, the power of illusion and sleep. Thomas Colburn discusses the relevance of the Goddess:

> To her are ascribed the powers of creation, maintenance and destruc tion that in other narrative and

theological settings belong to the three gods Brahma, Vishnu and Shiva. They are her powers, because she is understood as the shakti, the interior power, the essential efficacy, of all that exists ... The Great Goddess is a unitary phenomenon but is also understood to be a dialectical paradox contained within that unity; she is both illusion (maya) and the knowledge that dispels it, has both gentle and terrible forms, is both benign and martial, is both poles of any polarity, including reality and unreality. There is nothing extrinsic to her.[6]

Himalaya gave her a lion to ride upon and various jewels. (2.13.17, 19-20, 28)7

When Devi appeared before Mahishasura on the battleground in her towering form, his army of asuras began its assault from all sides. With her ten arms wielding the weapons of the celestials and immortal gods, Devi deftly slaughtered them all. The great demon warrior Raktabija came forward to challenge the Goddess.

As Kali, Devi slaughtered Raktabija's army and then entreated him to battle; with every injury she inflicted on the demon, drops of blood fell to the

ground. Each drop manifested into another warrior, and soon she was surrounded by many enormous figures, which she devoured instantly. Then, to overcome the demons, she would pierce their bodies and drink every last drop of blood. Soon Raktabija was rendered senseless and exhausted by the fury of battle, at which time Devi slew him mercilessly and then began to dance.

Mahishasura, who had the ability to change his form at will, approached the Goddess in multiple manifestations, appearing as a buffalo, an elephant and then a bull. Devi skillfully defeated the demon and reveled in her divine, wrathful mood.

Her dance of fury and destruction shook the worlds, throwing the gods and all living beings into terror. The earth shook and mountains swayed. It appeared that all of the worlds were to dissolve at any moment. Nothing could take her out of this trance as she was intoxicated by the awesome manifestation of her prowess. None but Shiva dared approach her at this time. To pacify and release her from this state, Shiva lay down beneath her in the form of a corpse and she began to dance on his form. When she awoke form the trance and understood that she was standing above her beloved, her mood changed and she stretched out her tongue in shame. Thus, the world was saved from her destructive manifestation.

Kinsley narrates the third division of the text:

> Kali's most famous appearances in battle contexts are found in the Devi Mahatmya. In the third episode, which features Durga's defeat of Sumbha and Nisumbha and their allies, Kali appears twice. Early in the battle the demons Canda and Munda approach Durga with readied weapons. Seeing them prepared to attack her, Durga becomes angry, her face becoming dark as ink. Suddenly the goddess

Kali springs from her forehead. She is black, wears a garland of human heads and a tiger skin and wields a skill-topped staff. She is gaunt, with sunken eyes, gaping mouth and lolling tongue. She roars loudly and leaps into the battle, where she tears demons apart with her hands and crushes them in her jaws. She grasps the two demon generals and in one furious blow decapitates them both with her sword.(7.3-22)[8]

In the next three divisions of this text, the three major functions of the Goddess are characterized; Mahakali, Mahalakshmi, and Mahasaraswati are symbolically figured in the narrative cycles respectively.[9] Kali is destruction and transformation. Lakshmi is abundance, prosperity and beauty. Saraswati is wisdom, enlightenment and the divine word. Together they form a comprehensive vision of reality and the relationship between the divine feminine and the self in its journey through life. ■

The Goddess and Tantra

The worship of the Goddess as Shakti is involved with the spiritual path of Tantra. Tantra is a broad subject, and tantric scriptures as they appear in India come from three sources: Vaishnava Agamas (Pancharatra), Shaivite Agamas and Shakta Agamas. The latter is the basis of what is most commonly referred to as Tantric scripture, as Shaktism is most prominent in tantric groups. Fundamentally, they all deal with at least five universal aspects of existence: creation, maintenance, and destruction of the cosmos, as well as the bondage and enlightenment of the individual.

The path of Tantra has as its goal the full realization of all aspects of the self and ultimately liberation. Tantra, with its basis deep in samkhya, or Vedic cosmology, recognizes the world and the psycho-physical organism as the ground of awakening. As opposed to the doctrines of classical yoga outlined in the yoga-sutra of Patanjali, wherein the aspirant seeks a total separation of the conscious principle from manifest

nature, Tantra rests on the metaphysical view of Shiva/Shakti. This integral worldview recognizes the eternal or inseparable union of both masculine and feminine principles, or of substance and form, spirit and nature. Through the use of mudras (symbolic gestures), mantras (cosmic diagrams) and yantras (divine forms for visualization and identification), the practitioner engages in ritual contemplative practices that transform both the psychic and physical aspects of the self. Through the grace of the Goddess and arduous effort on behalf of the initiate, transcendent wisdom awakens in one's experience, harmonizing the dual nature of reality.

It is not the world that is to be rejected, but the fundamental misapprehension of the self and ignorance of the intrinsic sacredness of the world. These two illusions inhibit a full realization of one's spiritual existence and personality.[10] In this last age of the cosmos' four cycles, the Kali Yuga, the path of Tantra and worship of the Goddess become especially relevant, according to the tradition. The religion of the Vedas, established in ritualism, and the world-denying Upanishadic trend both become less relevant and practical in a world situation that requires enlightened involvement. In certain forms of Shakta Tantrism, the practices of yoga are incorporated with devotion to the Goddess. She is worshipped in her manifestation of the ten Mahavidyas, ten tanctric aspects of the Goddess.[11]

David Kingsley's work on the Goddess in Hindu mythology discusses the origin of the Mahavidyas:

> The origin of the ten Mahavidyas in Hindu Mythology takes place in the context of the story of Sati and Shiva. Sati's father, Daksha, decides to perform a great sacrifice and invites all the inhabitants of the heavenly spheres to attend ... Shiva is not pleased to hear this and forbids her to attend the sacrifice. Sati is

unable to change Shiva's mind and eventually loses her temper. First she assumes a dreadful form, and then she multiplies herself into ten forms, the Muhavidyas: Kali, Tara, Chinnamasta, Bhuvaneshvari, Bagala, Dhumavati, Kamala, Matangi, Sodashi and Bhairavi.[12] ■

Other Aspects of the Goddess

Devi is also realized in her personified aspects within nature. As Mother Earth, she is Bhumi, who is known to supplicate Brahma and Vishnu to alleviate the sufferings of all beings burdered by demonic influences or the self-destructive tendencies of man. She is Ganga, daughter of the Himalayas and also the Goddess Saraswati, who descend in the forms of holy rivers. Her waters purify pilgrims of their karma and bestow devotion and enlightenment.

Saraswati's most familiar role is as the patron goddess of the arts, music and learning. She presides over sound and is related to Vach, the goddess of speech. She is most commonly depicted holding a vine and surrounded by the swan and lotus, both symbols of purity. In these forms, the Goddess embodies the revelatory aspect of divinity and brings forth auspiciousness and wisdom into the world. Transcendent wisdom is conscious and personal; the Vedas and Upanishads themselves are characterized as divine personalities in many scriptures.

The sapta matrikas, or seven aspects of the divine mother, are worshipped in local shrines throughout India. The mythological basis of their manifestation is related to the battle of Devi with Sumbha and Nisumbha in the third episode of the Devi Mahatmya.[13]

When the demon armies approach her, the male gods, who are watching from the sidelines, create shaktis, female counterparts of themselves, to help Devi on the battlefield. Seven such shaktis are created, and in appearance Brahmani, created from the god Brahma, holds a rosary and water pot; Maheshvari, created from

Shiva, is seated on a bull, and holds a trident, wears serpent bracelets, and is adorned with a crescent moon; Kaumari, created from Kartikkeya, rides a peacock and holds a spear; Vaishnavi, created from Vishnu, is seated on Garuda and holds a conch, chakra (discus), mace, bow and sword; Varahi, created from the boar avatara of Vishnu, has the form of a boar; Narasimhi, created from the man-lion avatara of Vishnu, has the form of a woman-lion and throws the stars into disarray with the shaking of her lion's mane; and Aindri, created from the god Indra, holds a thunderbolt and is seated

The Matrikas are primarily an independent group of goddesses who have violent natures, are associated with diseases, and are particularly prone to afflict small children. Many local or village goddesses are also associated with diseases, and are particularly prone to afflict small children. They are routinely served with blood, and are held to have violent natures. It is quite likely that the Matrikas of the Hindu literary tradition, beginning with the Mahabharata, can be identified with those goddesses, who are so central to the religious life of most Hindu villages.[15] ■

Devi: Dynamic Force of Love

The fundamental nature of the Goddess is her love; her many manifestations are expressions of that dynamic force. We learn of her love through nature as she brings about circumstances so that we may question our pain. She provides us with pleasurable situations only to snatch them from our grip, thus releasing us from our fascination with short-lived and

illusory things. Then we are left to search for that beauty and love which she alone can ultimately reveal to us. The immortal character of such love can free us from our worldly passions. ■

Notes:

1. Dehejia, *Encountering Devi*, p. 13

2. Jung. *The Archetypes and the Collective Unconscious*, p. 92

3. McDermott, Rachel Fell. *The Western Kali* in *Devi: Goddess of India*. p. 293.

4. Danielou. *The Myths and Gods of India*, pp. 271–273.

5. Kinsley, p. 102.

6. Colburn in *Devi*, p. 42.

7. Colburn in *Devi*, p. 44.

8. Kinsley, pp. 118.

9. Kinsley, pp. 107 – 109.

10. For an authoritive discussion of Tantra see Feuerstein, *Tantra: the Path of Ecstasy*.

11. For a general overview of the Mahavidyas see Frawley, *Tantric Yoga and the Wisdom Goddesses*.

12. Kinsley, p. 163.

13. Kinsley, pp. 151–160.

14. Kinsley, p. 156.

15. Kinsley, p. 160.

The Iconography of the Lakshmi Image

Lakshmi, the goddess of fortune, is depicted with lotus in hand. The lotus is a symbol for purity and perfection as well as fertility. Thus she is known as Padma or Kamala, "the Lady of the Lotus". She is also known as Sri, the goddess of beauty.

The Iconography of the Kali Image

Kali, the dark one, is represented with four arms. In one hand she bears a sword by which she cuts the knots of illusion which bind all souls; in the other she holds the head of a demon representing our release from a limited sense of self. Her other two arms bestow blessing (varada) and fearlessness (abhaya) to her devotees. Often she is shown adorned in a garland of skulls, almost completely nude and with three red eyes andprotruding tongue. Her darkness and nudity reveal her infinitude, her awe-inspiring form speaks of a mother archetype, which is both fertile, destructive and wondrous.

The Iconography of the Saraswati Image

Saraswati is the goddess of revelation: of song, myth, art and learning and is thus related to Vach, the goddess of speech. She is most often depicted seated on a lotus, accompanied by her swan which both symbolize her beauty and purity. She is depicted holding the vina (lute) on which she plays the immortal sounds of the Vedas and bears a mala (rosary), book and water pot. She is the goddess of the rite, of spiritual practices and knowledge.